About the Book

Have you ever gone outside and thought you were all alone? Look around you, look carefully. Animals, fish, birds, and insects have developed means of protection that are meant to deceive. Wilda Ross gives us an understanding of how some animals are protected by camouflage in this informative, clearly written text. With this knowledge you may find a mouse hiding in the shadow of a log, a moth resting on the bark of a tree, a crab camouflaged by seaweed, or a katydid that looks just like a leaf.

Wilda Ross has written two books in the *Science Is What and Why* series, *What Did the Dinosaurs Eat?* and *Who Lives in This Log?* She was graduated from the University of California at Berkeley with a degree in botany. She has taught classes and written articles for the San Francisco *Examiner* on natural history. Wilda Ross makes her home in Mill Valley, California, where she continues her study of animal life and photography.

John Hamberger drew the colorful and realistic illustrations for this book. He is a well-known children's book illustrator who particularly enjoys drawing animals. He has paintings on permanent exhibit in the Museum of Natural History in New York and is a winner of the Christophers Award for his illustrations in *Vanishing Wings*. Mr. Hamberger lives in New York City but spends as much time as possible on his Camptown, Pennsylvania, farm.

COWARD, McCANN & GEOGHEGAN, INC.
NEW YORK

CAN YOU FIND THE
ANIMAL?

by WILDA ROSS • pictures by JOHN HAMBERGER

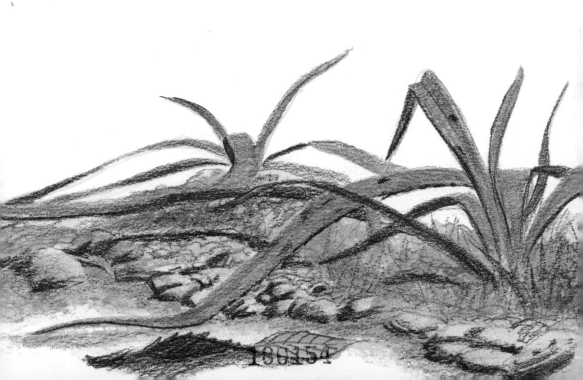

General Editor: Margaret Farrington Bartlett
Consultant: Theodore D. Johnson
Montclair Public Schools

Can you find the moth resting
on the bark of this tree?
It is hidden from the bird hunting for food.
The hungry bird is in too much of a hurry
to notice the moth.

If the bird took more time,
as you are doing,
it would see the shape of the moth.

It is hard to see
because the dark, wavy lines
on the wings of the moth
run into the same kind of lines on the bark.

Spots, lines, and stripes on an animal's body
help it to blend into its surroundings.
This way of hiding while still being
in full view is called camouflage.

While hunting for their food,
many animals have to keep
from being eaten themselves.
They can either run, fly, swim, or not be seen.
If the moth had moved even a little bit,
the bird would have seen it.

Stillness is an important part of full-view hiding.
Nesting birds not only blend into the background,
but must stay very still
as much of the time as possible.

If danger threatens a bittern feeding in a
marsh, it will stand straight and stiff.
The long brown stripes on its breast look
like the colors and shapes of the marsh plants.

When a breeze blows the reeds,
the bittern will sway back and forth.
The camouflage makes him
look like swaying marsh plants.
Can you find two bitterns?

11

An Eskimo can often see
the shadow of a polar bear
on the snow from a long distance.
Its shadow hardly shows if the bear lies
down in the snow.
Many animals lie flat or crouch while resting.
Some have special ways
of making their shadows smaller.

13

The wings of this moth are so thin that
it has no shadow when the wings are pressed
against the bark. As it raises its wings
to fly, the shadow appears.

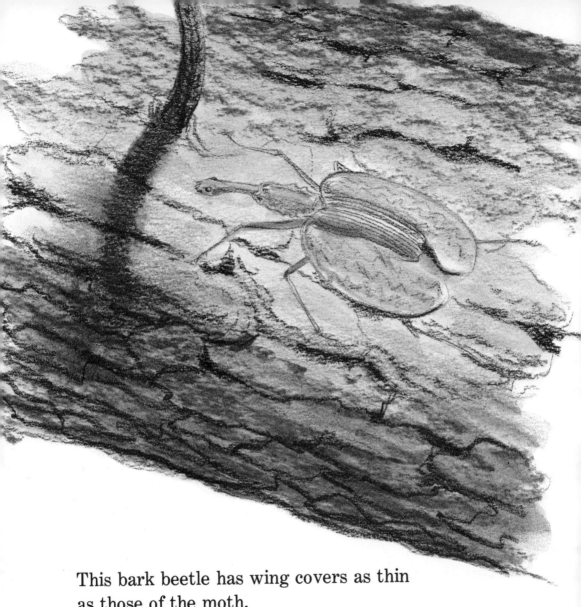

This bark beetle has wing covers as thin
as those of the moth.
The wing covers serve only to flatten the body
and lessen the shadow.
They do not help the beetle to fly.

Deer, rabbits, mice, and many other defenseless animals have another way of hiding themselves.

The darkest part of a deer is the back,
and the under parts are lighter.
Shade from its own body blends
with the color of the deer
and helps it look like forest shadows.

Fish are often dark blue on the back,
shading to silver on the sides.
Their outlines blend
into the dark water below.

Animals without color
such as jellyfish, prawns, and young fish
live near the surface of the ocean.
Light passes through their bodies,
making them difficult to see.

A garbage-heap kind of camouflage
is used by some crabs and insects.
The masking crab covers its shell
with bits of seaweed or sponges.

Stiff hairs with hooked tips
cover the crab's shell.
It hooks the bits of seaweed onto the hairs
with its pincers.

Fish like to eat caddis worms
when they can find them crawling on a stream bed.
When caddis worms are still, they look
like part of the bottom of the stream.

The caddis worm also uses the garbage
kind of camouflage in a skillful way.
It spins a silken tube about its body,
closing one end.
Then it fastens bits of dead leaves and twigs
to the outside of the tube with more silken threads.
When resting, the caddis worm
pulls its head and legs back into the tube.

A small pile of dead insects sticking
to a leaf may not be just forest litter.
Watch it. Does it move?
The larva of a green lacewing may be underneath.

After the lacewing sucks out the insect juices,
it fastens their dead bodies into hairs
covering its back.
This disguise will help
the lacewing catch more insects and escape being seen.

Does anybody see a katydid in this picture?
This member of the grasshopper family is
an example of one of the best kinds of camouflage
because it looks almost like a leaf.

If the katydid stays still, a hungry bird
will mistake it for a leaf, almost every time.
Some katydids have spots or notches that look
like leaves that have been chewed by caterpillars.

The leaf fish of South America
either hangs with its head down
under the surface of the water
or lies still at the bottom of the river
among rotting leaves.
When caught in a net,
it continues to play "dead."

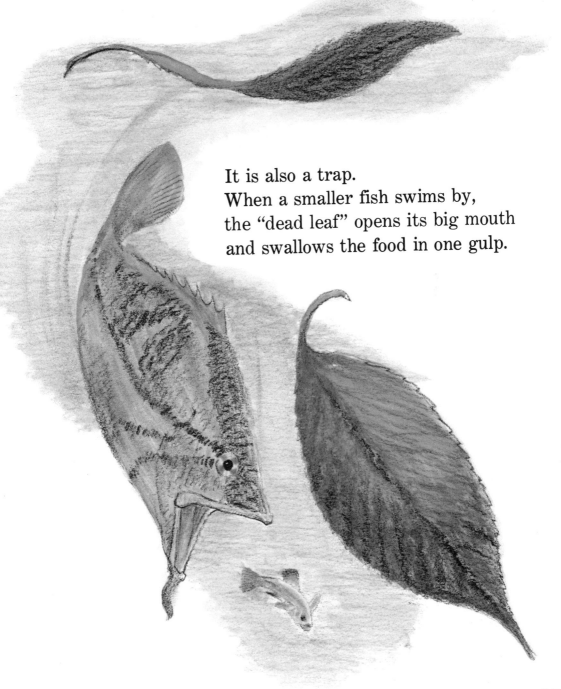

It is also a trap.
When a smaller fish swims by,
the "dead leaf" opens its big mouth
and swallows the food in one gulp.

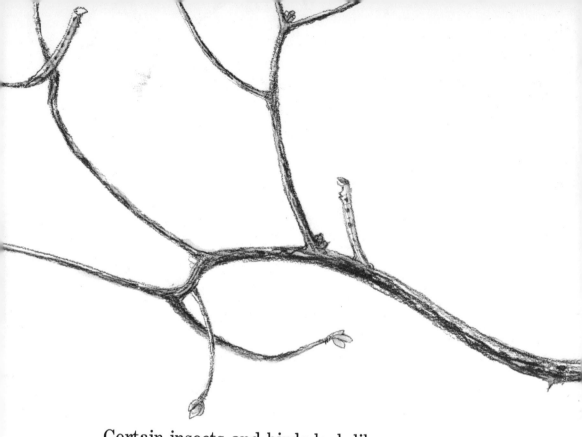

Certain insects and birds look like
thorns, twigs, or grass stems.
While resting on a branch,
the measuring worm caterpillar holds the back end
of its gray body out like a twig.
When a measuring worm crawls about,
it picks up one end at a time because it has
no legs in the middle of its body
as most caterpillars do.
Can you find seven measuring worms?

You may never see a walking stick insect
because it looks so much like
the twigs of trees and shrubs
on which it lives.

Like many other plant eaters, walking sticks
move very slowly. They drop their eggs,
which look like seeds, onto the leaf-covered ground.
In the spring the eggs hatch and the babies
crawl up on the plants around them.
Do you see two on this branch?

Can you find an insect in the pink orchid flower?
It is waiting for a bee,
or maybe a butterfly, to land there.

Suddenly, before the butterfly can correct its mistake,
the female mantis has grabbed it
in her spiny front legs.
She slowly chews her food as if it were a ripe banana.

The oceans are full of animals
that look like plants.
Broad-leaved seaweeds growing in shallow water
make especially good hiding places
for pipefish and sea horses.

These fish swim upright
and rest among the seaweeds,
gently swaying with the motion of the plants.
There are two pipefish and two sea horses in this picture.

An animal's color is usually part of its outer covering.
It may be fur, feather, horny skin, or scales.
The colors change very little
after the animal dies.

Sea slugs, however, are the same colors as the
sponges and seaweeds they eat because the color
becomes part of their bodies.
When they die, their bodies quickly turn brown
like a dead piece of seaweed.

Can you find two sea slugs?

Most animals are born with their camouflage colors.
Those whose colors do not match
their background closely enough
are quickly seen and eaten.

Certain moths that rest on
the bark of trees in city parks
used to be light gray to match the tree bark.
Bits of soot from the city's smoke-filled air
collect on the tree trunks and slowly darken them.
Now that kind of moth is the color of smoke.

The light gray moths have become
the easiest for the birds to find.
Before these moths have time
to lay their eggs, birds eat them.

If we continue to fill our city air with smoke,
all the trees will have smoky trunks
and all the moths will be that color too.

Now that you know some ways animals avoid being eaten,
you will see more when you go outdoors.
Watch quietly.
Can you find any animals
being protected by camouflage?

INDEX

ℛ